How to Flip Houses for Massive Profits

The Step-By-Step Playbook For Scoring Deals, Fixing Up Properties, and Making 6 Figures on Your First Deal

The Fix-It Guy

Table of Contents

Introduction

Welcome, future real estate moguls and aspiring house-flipping extraordinaires! If you've ever dreamed of turning rundown properties into pockets full of cash, you're in the right place. Grab a seat, because we're about to embark on a thrilling journey through the world of house flipping, where fortunes are made, dreams are realized, and savvy investors reign supreme.

Ever wondered how some folks turn a dilapidated fixer-upper into a six-figure jackpot on their very first deal? Well, buckle up because "How to Flip Houses for Massive Profits" is your backstage pass to the ultimate playbook for success. I'm not here to sugarcoat, it's going to be challenging, it's going to be intense, but by the end of this journey, you'll be equipped with the knowledge and strategies to transform your real estate aspirations into a lucrative reality.

Picture this: You, standing on the steps of a newly renovated property, a sold sign swinging in the breeze, and a fat check in your hand, all because you cracked the code to profitable house flipping. Whether you're a seasoned investor looking to up your game or a rookie itching for that first deal, this book is your roadmap to scoring deals, revamping properties, and hitting that sweet spot of six figures on your very first flip.

But, hey, I get it. The real estate game can be daunting. It's not just about buying low and selling high; it's about strategy, team-building, and a dash of fearless tenacity. In these pages, I'm not just going to tell you what to do, I'm going to show you how to do it, step by step, with real-life examples and insider tips that the pros don't always share.

So, are you ready to turn your passion for real estate into a profit-pumping venture? Are you prepared to roll up your sleeves and transform properties into gold mines? If the answer is a resounding "Yes!" then let's dive in together. Your journey to massive profits begins right here, right now. Get ready to flip the script on your financial future.

Chapter 1

Getting Started

Assessing Your Readiness

Alright, future property tycoons, it's time to kick off this adventure. I know, I know, diving into the world of house flipping can feel like standing on the edge of a high dive, contemplating the plunge. But fear not, because I'm here to be your guide, your real estate Yoda, if you will.

Assessing Your Readiness

Step 1: Take Stock of Your Passion
Let's begin with a gut check. Ask yourself, "Am I ready for this wild ride?" House flipping isn't just about making a quick buck; it's about passion and commitment. If you're not in it for the long haul, you might as well stick to Monopoly. So, grab a notepad, jot down your reasons, and make sure they're as solid as the foundation of the house you're about to flip.

Troubleshooting Tip: Feeling a bit shaky on the commitment front? Break it down. List the benefits you'll reap from successful flips. It's like a pep talk from yourself to yourself.

Step 2: Assess Your Financial Fitness

No one likes talking about money, but let's face it, you're not going to flip houses with pocket change. Take a hard look at your finances. What's your budget? How much can you realistically invest without selling a kidney? Be honest with yourself; this is the starting point for your journey.

Troubleshooting Tip: If your budget is more Ramen-noodle than champagne dreams, fear not. There are creative financing options, and we'll dive into those later. Just keep an open mind, and remember, Rome wasn't flipped in a day.

Step 3: Time, Talent, and Tenacity Check

Now, let's talk about the three Ts, time, talent, and tenacity. Do you have the time to commit to this venture? Are you a DIY whiz or will you need a squad of experts? And most importantly, do you have the tenacity to weather the storms that come with flipping? It's not all sunshine and granite countertops, my friend.

Troubleshooting Tip: If time feels like your mortal enemy, don't panic. We'll discuss strategies to optimize your efforts and maybe even bend time a little.

Key Takeaways

- Passion is your fuel; without it, you'll run out of gas.
- Money matters, so know your budget like the back of your hand.
- Assess your time, talent, and tenacity, it's a triple threat.

Next Steps

1. Reflect on your passion. Are you in this for the right reasons?
2. Crunch the numbers. What's your budget?
3. Evaluate your time, talent, and tenacity. Can you commit?

Remember, this is just the beginning. Strap in, because we're just getting warmed up!

Defining Your Investment Goals

Hey there, future real estate moguls! Now that we've laid the groundwork in Chapter 1, it's time to zoom in on something crucial: your investment goals. Think of this chapter as the GPS for your house-flipping journey. Without a destination, you might end up in a maze of confusion. So, grab a cup of coffee, find a comfy seat, and let's hash out those goals.

Start by Dreaming Big

Step 1: Picture Your Ideal Outcome
Close your eyes and envision the perfect scenario. What does success look like for you? Is it a fat check in your hand after selling a renovated gem? Maybe it's building a real estate empire? Whatever it is, paint that mental picture. We're not just flipping houses; we're crafting your dream.

Troubleshooting Tip: If you're drawing a blank, no worries. Flip through some real estate magazines, binge-watch HGTV, and let the inspiration flow. Your vision will come to you.

Set SMART Goals

Step 2: Make Your Goals SMART

Now that you have the dream, let's make it tangible. SMART goals are Specific, Measurable, Achievable, Relevant, and Time-bound. Instead of saying, "I want to make money," say, "I aim to profit $100,000 within 12 months by flipping two properties in my local market." See the difference? SMART goals turn dreams into action plans.

Troubleshooting Tip: Feeling overwhelmed by the specifics? Break it down. Start small, and as you gain confidence, your goals can grow.

Balance Risk and Reward

Step 3: Assess Your Risk Tolerance

Let's talk risk. Every venture comes with a bit of uncertainty, but how much risk can you stomach? Are you a thrill-seeker or more of a cautious calculator? Knowing your risk tolerance helps you navigate the unpredictable waves of the real estate sea.

Troubleshooting Tip: If risk feels like a four-letter word, it's okay. We'll explore strategies to minimize risk and keep you comfortable.

Key Takeaways

- Visualize your dream outcome to set the stage for success.
- Make your goals SMART for a clear roadmap.
- Assess your risk tolerance to navigate the real estate rollercoaster.

Next Steps

1. Envision your ideal outcome. What does success look like?
2. Make your goals SMART. Get specific!
3. Assess your risk tolerance. How comfortable are you with the unknown?

Now that your goals are crystal clear, get ready to turn those dreams into reality. The real estate adventure continues!

Creating a Realistic Budget

Think of this chapter as your financial compass, it's going to guide you through the twists and turns of real estate finance. So, roll up those sleeves, grab your favorite calculator, and let's dive in.

Know Your Numbers

Step 1: Break Down Your Costs
Flipping houses is like planning a wedding, you need to know where every dollar is going. Start by listing all potential expenses: purchase price, renovation costs, permits, labor, holding costs, and, of course, the occasional pizza for your hardworking crew. The more detailed, the better.

Troubleshooting Tip: If numbers make your head spin, take a deep breath. We'll break it down into bite-sized chunks.

Step 2: Factor in Contingencies
Reality check: things rarely go as planned. Unexpected hiccups, delays, and surprise expenses are all part of the game. So, pad your budget with a contingency fund, think of it as the financial equivalent of an umbrella for a rainy day. Trust me; you'll thank yourself later.

Troubleshooting Tip: Worried about overspending? We'll discuss strategies to keep your budget in check without sacrificing quality.

Get Creative with Financing

Step 3: Explore Financing Options

Unless you've struck oil in your backyard, you'll likely need some financial backing. From traditional mortgages to private loans, there's a smorgasbord of options. Choose the one that fits your budget and goals.

Troubleshooting Tip: If the world of loans feels like a maze, I get it. We'll break it down into a friendly neighborhood stroll.

Key Takeaways
- Break down costs to the last nail and tile.
- Embrace the unexpected with a contingency fund.
- Explore financing options that align with your budget and goals.

Next Steps
1. List all potential expenses. Get granular!
2. Add a contingency fund to your budget. Expect the unexpected.
3. Explore financing options that suit your budget and goals.

Chapter 2

Building Your Team

Finding the Right Real Estate Agent

Now that we've nailed down your goals and budget, it's time to assemble your dream team. And what's a dream team without the star player? In the world of house flipping, that MVP is your real estate agent. This chapter is all about finding the right Sherlock Holmes to your Watson, the yin to your yang, the real estate agent who will be your trusted guide through the labyrinth of property deals.

Understand Their Superpower

Step 1: Recognize the Power of a Good Agent
A great real estate agent is like a wizard with a bag of tricks. They know the market like the back of their hand, have a sixth sense for upcoming opportunities and can negotiate deals that make your wallet do a happy dance. Find someone who's not just about closing deals but is genuinely invested in your success.

Troubleshooting Tip: If you're thinking, "But how do I find this mythical creature?" fear not. We'll break down the qualities to look for in your real estate soulmate.

Seek Local Expertise

Step 2: Local Know-How is Key
Your ideal agent should be a walking, talking encyclopedia of the local real estate scene. They know the neighborhoods, the school districts, the coffee shops with the best muffins, everything. Why? Because this knowledge is gold when it comes to picking the right properties for your flips.

Troubleshooting Tip: Feeling lost in a sea of real estate jargon? We'll provide a cheat sheet, so you can talk the talk with your agent.

Chemistry Matters

Step 3: Find Your Real Estate BFF
This might sound touchy-feely, but it's crucial. You're not just hiring an agent; you're entering a partnership. Find someone whose communication style aligns with yours, someone you trust to have your back when the stakes are high. Chemistry is the secret sauce for a successful agent-investor relationship.

Troubleshooting Tip: If you're thinking, "I have better chemistry with my morning coffee," don't worry. We'll discuss how to build that rapport.

Key Takeaways
- A good agent is your secret weapon in the real estate game.
- Local expertise is a non-negotiable quality.
- Chemistry with your agent is the glue that holds your partnership together.

Next Steps
1. Define what you need in an agent. Make a wish list!
2. Look for local experts with a proven track record.
3. Meet potential agents and trust your gut. Chemistry is key.

Ready to find your real estate soulmate? Let's hit the streets and uncover the Sherlock Holmes of your flipping adventure in the next section!

Hiring a Competent Contractor

Greetings, future property transformers! Now that you've secured the Watson to your Sherlock (your real estate agent), it's time to enlist the craftsman, the magician of hammers and nails, the contractor. In this chapter, we're diving into the art of hiring a competent contractor, the maestro who will turn your fixer-upper into a jaw-dropping masterpiece.

Craftsmanship Comes First

Step 1: Prioritize Skill and Experience
Think of your contractor as the conductor of a symphony. You want someone who knows their instruments inside out. Look for a contractor with a proven track record, a portfolio that speaks volumes, and a reputation for delivering quality craftsmanship.

Troubleshooting Tip: If the world of construction feels like a foreign language, fear not. We'll decode it, so you can speak with the contractor with confidence.

Check Their Credentials

Step 2: Verify Licenses and Insurance
Imagine hiring a chef without checking if they've got the right ingredients. Similarly, don't skip the due diligence with your contractor. Ensure they have the necessary licenses and insurance. This isn't just paperwork; it's your safety net against unexpected twists in your flipping journey.

Troubleshooting Tip: If the thought of navigating contractor paperwork gives you a headache, I've got your back. We'll break it down into a simple checklist.

Communication is Key

Step 3: Look for Effective Communication
Ever tried playing charades with a contractor? Spoiler alert: it's not fun. Your contractor should be a clear communicator. They need to understand your vision and update you on progress without turning it into a Shakespearean drama.

Troubleshooting Tip: If you're thinking, "I just want to avoid miscommunications," we're on the same page. We'll discuss strategies to keep the lines of communication crystal clear.

Key Takeaways
- Prioritize skill and experience in your contractor search.
- Verify licenses and insurance for a secure partnership.
- Effective communication is non-negotiable.

Next Steps
1. List the skills and experience you want in a contractor.
2. Check credentials, licenses and insurance are a must.
3. Meet potential contractors and gauge their communication style.

Ready to turn your vision into reality with a skilled contractor by your side? Onward to the next step in building your A-team!

Assembling a Reliable Support Team

Hey, aspiring property magicians! Now that you've found your real estate agent and a top-notch contractor, it's time to expand your crew. This chapter is all about building a support team that will make your house-flipping venture a symphony of success. Think of it as assembling the Avengers, each member with a unique skill set to conquer the challenges ahead.

The Financial Sidekick: Accountant or Financial Advisor

Step 1: Bring in the Number Cruncher
Numbers can be the hero or villain of your flipping saga. A skilled accountant or financial advisor is your financial sidekick, ensuring you stay on budget, maximize profits, and navigate the tax landscape without breaking a sweat.

Troubleshooting Tip: If numbers make you break into a cold sweat, don't worry. We'll explore how to find a financial guru who speaks your language.

The Legal Eagle: Real Estate Attorney

Step 2: Enlist the Legal Jedi

Every superhero needs a lawyer, and in the real estate world, that's your real estate attorney. They'll help you navigate contracts, review agreements, and make sure you're on the right side of the law throughout your house-flipping adventure.

Troubleshooting Tip: Legal jargon got you scratching your head? We'll simplify it into plain English.

The Marketing Maestro: Home Stager or Marketing Specialist

Step 3: Amp Up Your Marketing Game

To sell a house, you need to make it irresistible. Enter the home stager or marketing specialist. They'll help you showcase your flip in the best light, ensuring potential buyers fall head over heels.

Troubleshooting Tip: If you think marketing is a foreign language, you're not alone. We'll unravel the mysteries of effective property promotion.

Key Takeaways
- Your support team is your real estate Avengers, each member has a unique role.
- A financial sidekick ensures your numbers are the heroes, not villains.
- A legal Jedi keeps you on the right side of the law.
- A marketing maestro makes your properties irresistible.

Next Steps
1. Identify the skills your support team needs.
2. Find a financial sidekick, legal Jedi, and marketing maestro who aligns with your goals.
3. Build relationships with each team member for a seamless partnership.

Congratulations! You're now one step closer to having a powerhouse team that will elevate your house-flipping game. Stay tuned for the next chapter as we delve into the art of scouting lucrative deals!

Building a support team that will make your house-flipping venture a symphony of success.

Chapter 3

Scouting Lucrative Deals

Identifying Potential Properties

Hey savvy property hunters! Now that your dream team is in place, it's time to dive into the exciting realm of finding those diamonds in the rough. This chapter is your treasure map, guiding you through the process of identifying potential properties that could be the golden ticket to your next successful flip.

Know Your Niche

Step 1: Define Your Target Market

Imagine trying to catch a fish without knowing what kind of fish you're after. Likewise, understanding your target market is crucial. Are you flipping family homes, trendy condos, or historic fixer-uppers? Knowing your niche helps you tailor your search and maximize your profits.

Troubleshooting Tip: If you're unsure about your niche, we'll explore ways to identify the sweet spot that aligns with your goals.

Embrace the Art of Research

Step 2: Dive into Research
Now, put on your detective hat and grab your magnifying glass. Research is your secret weapon. Dive into local market trends, property values, and neighborhood dynamics. The more you know, the better equipped you are to spot those hidden gems.

Troubleshooting Tip: If research sounds overwhelming, don't stress. We'll break it down into manageable chunks.

Develop a Keen Eye for Potential

Step 3: Spot the Diamond in the Rough
Ever seen an episode of your favorite home renovation show and thought, "How did they see the potential in that mess?" It's an acquired skill. Train your eyes to see beyond the worn carpet and dated wallpaper. Look for properties with good bones, in need of a little love, but with the potential to shine.

Troubleshooting Tip: If you're struggling to see potential, fear not. We'll discuss practical strategies to identify diamonds in the rough.

Key Takeaways
- Define your target market to tailor your property search.
- Dive into research to understand local market dynamics.
- Develop a keen eye for spotting the potential in properties.

Next Steps
1. Define your target market. What types of properties align with your goals?
2. Dive into research. Know your local market like the back of your hand.
3. Train your eyes to spot potential. Look beyond surface flaws.

Get ready to embark on a thrilling adventure of property hunting. The next chapter awaits, where we'll delve into analyzing market trends to further sharpen your deal-scouting skills!

Analyzing Market Trends

Hello, future property trendsetters! Now that you've honed your skills in identifying potential properties, it's time to add a touch of clairvoyance to your toolkit. This chapter is all about analyzing market trends, the crystal ball that will help you predict where the real estate winds are blowing. Get ready to become the trend whisperer!

Step 1: Understand Seasonal Trends
Every market dances to its beat, and knowing the seasonal rhythms is your backstage pass. Are spring sales blooming? Do winter months slow down? Understanding these patterns helps you time your flips for maximum impact.

Troubleshooting Tip: If seasonal trends feel like a mystery, don't worry. We'll unravel the seasons of the real estate market.

Step 2: Keep an Eye on Neighborhood Developments
Neighborhoods are like living organisms, they evolve. Stay vigilant for signs of revitalization or decline. New schools, trendy cafes, or major infrastructure projects can turn a forgotten area into the next hot spot.

Troubleshooting Tip: If deciphering neighborhood developments feels like reading tea leaves, we'll guide you through the process.

Step 3: Dive into Data Analysis
Numbers are the breadcrumbs that lead to real estate gold. Explore data on property values, market saturation, and local demographics. This data dance will reveal patterns that can guide your investment decisions.

Troubleshooting Tip: If you're not a data whiz, fear not. We'll demystify the data dance and make it a breeze.

Key Takeaways
- Understand seasonal trends to time your flips strategically.
- Keep an eye on neighborhood developments for potential hotspots.
- Dive into data analysis to uncover valuable market insights.

Next Steps
1. Research seasonal trends in your market.
2. Stay informed about neighborhood developments.
3. Dive into data analysis. What do the numbers say about your target area?

Negotiating the Best Deals

Greetings, future deal-makers! Now that you've identified the perfect property and are well-versed in market trends, it's time to step into the negotiating arena. This chapter is your crash course in the art of negotiation, a skill that can be the difference between a profitable flip and a missed opportunity. Get ready to channel your inner negotiator!

Know Your Numbers Inside Out

Step 1: Establish Your Walk-Away Point
Before entering negotiations, set a firm walk-away point. Knowing the maximum you're willing to pay ensures you don't get swept away in the heat of the moment. It's your financial compass in the negotiation jungle.

Troubleshooting Tip: If setting a walk-away point feels like a daunting task, we'll guide you through the process.

Create Win-Win Scenarios

Step 2: Seek Mutually Beneficial Solutions
Negotiation is not a zero-sum game. Aim for win-win scenarios where both parties walk away satisfied. This approach builds goodwill and can lead to future opportunities and positive relationships.

Troubleshooting Tip: If the idea of win-win seems idealistic, fear not. We'll explore practical strategies to achieve balance in negotiations.

Master the Art of Communication

Step 3: Hone Your Communication Skills
Effective communication is the heart of negotiation. Listen actively, ask probing questions, and be clear in expressing your needs. Understanding the other party's motivations gives you a powerful edge.

Troubleshooting Tip: If the thought of negotiating makes you break into a cold sweat, relax. We'll share communication hacks to boost your confidence.

Key Takeaways
- Establish a walk-away point before entering negotiations.
- Aim for win-win solutions to build positive relationships.
- Hone your communication skills for effective negotiation.

Next Steps

1. Set a firm walk-away point. What's your financial limit?
2. Aim for win-win scenarios in your negotiations.
3. Practice active listening and clear communication.

Congratulations! You're now armed with the tools to negotiate like a pro. The journey continues in the next chapter, where we'll unravel the intricate world of financing your flips. Get ready to explore the realm of loans, mortgages, and financial strategies!

Chapter 4

Financing Your Flips

Exploring Funding Options

Hello, financial trailblazers! Now that you've mastered the art of negotiation, let's tackle the financial frontier. This chapter is your compass through the vast landscape of funding options, a crucial step in turning your property dreams into a lucrative reality. Get ready to explore the diverse world of financing!

Assess Your Financial Landscape

Step 1: Know Your Financial Position
Before diving into funding options, take a thorough look at your financial landscape. What assets do you have? What's your credit score? Understanding your financial standing is the first step towards selecting the most suitable funding avenue.

Troubleshooting Tip: If assessing your finances feels overwhelming, worry not. We'll guide you through the process step by step.

Traditional Financing: Mortgages and Loans

Step 2: Dive into Traditional Options

Traditional financing, such as mortgages and loans, is a common path. Explore the world of lenders, interest rates, and repayment terms. Understanding these elements helps you navigate the sea of possibilities and choose the option that aligns with your goals.

Troubleshooting Tip: If the terminology sounds like a foreign language, relax. We'll provide a translator for your financial journey.

Alternative Paths: Private Lenders and Hard Money Loans

Step 3: Uncover Alternative Funding Routes

For the adventurous spirits, alternative financing options like private lenders and hard money loans can offer flexibility and speed. Dive into the details, weigh the risks, and discover whether these unconventional paths are the right fit for your flipping aspirations.

Troubleshooting Tip: If the world of alternative financing seems daunting, we're here to demystify it. We'll break it down into digestible chunks.

Key Takeaways

- Assess your financial position before exploring funding options.
- Understand traditional financing avenues like mortgages and loans.
- Explore alternative paths such as private lenders and hard money loans.

Next Steps

1. Assess your financial position. What assets do you have, and what's your credit score?
2. Understand traditional financing options—explore mortgages and loans.
3. Delve into alternative funding routes. Are private lenders or hard money loans the right fit?

Congratulations! You're now equipped to navigate the financial landscape of house flipping. The journey continues in the next chapter, where we'll tackle the legal intricacies of navigating the house-flipping process. Get ready for a crash course in permits, regulations, and legal considerations!

Understanding Loans and Mortgages

Greetings, financial trailblazers! Now that we're delving into the financial intricacies of house flipping, it's time to demystify two fundamental components: loans and mortgages. This chapter is your compass through the labyrinth of borrowing, interest rates, and repayment terms, a vital expedition in your quest for real estate riches.

Loans 101: Navigating the Basics

Step 1: Grasp the Fundamentals of Loans
Before diving into the mortgage maze, let's start with the basics. What is a loan, and how does it work? Loans involve borrowing a sum of money with the commitment to pay it back over time, often with interest. Understanding these fundamental principles sets the stage for exploring more complex financial tools.

Troubleshooting Tip: If the idea of loans feels overwhelming, take a breath. We'll break down the complexities into bite-sized pieces.

The Mortgage Map: Exploring Your Home Loan Options

Step 2: Navigate the Mortgage Landscape

Now, let's zoom in on mortgages, the cornerstone of real estate financing. Fixed-rate, adjustable-rate, FHA, VA, oh my! The mortgage world is a vast terrain with various options. Each type comes with its own set of advantages and considerations. We'll map out the landscape, helping you choose the mortgage that aligns with your flipping goals.

Troubleshooting Tip: If mortgage jargon leaves you scratching your head, worry not. We'll provide a glossary to decode the language of home loans.

Interest Rates and Repayment Plans: Decoding the Numbers

Step 3: Understand Interest Rates and Repayment Plans

Interest rates can feel like a mysterious force influencing your financial fate. In this section, we'll demystify interest rates and dissect various repayment plans. Whether fixed or adjustable, knowing the ins and outs empowers you to make informed decisions about your financial journey.

Troubleshooting Tip: If the thought of interest rates sends shivers down your spine, relax. We'll break it down into simple terms.

Key Takeaways

- Grasp the fundamentals of loans as the building blocks of financing.
- Navigate the mortgage landscape to find the loan that fits your goals.
- Understand interest rates and repayment plans to make informed financial decisions.

Next Steps

1. Get familiar with the basics of loans.
2. Explore the mortgage landscape, understand the different types.
3. Dive into interest rates and repayment plans. How do they impact your financial strategy?

Congratulations! You're now equipped with the knowledge to navigate the complex world of loans and mortgages. The journey continues in the next chapter, where we'll unravel the legal considerations that come with flipping houses. Get ready for a crash course in permits, regulations, and legal safeguards!

Your compass through the labyrinth of borrowing, interest rates, and repayment terms, a vital expedition in your quest for real estate riches.

Managing Financial Risks

Greetings, financial trailblazers! Now that we've explored the realms of loans and mortgages, it's time to equip ourselves with the armor needed to face financial risks head-on. This chapter is your guide to managing the uncertainties that come with house flipping, a crucial skill in steering your investment ship through turbulent waters.

Acknowledge the Risks

Step 1: Identify Potential Financial Pitfalls
The first step in managing financial risks is acknowledging their existence. From market fluctuations to unexpected renovation costs, understanding the potential pitfalls allows you to create a proactive plan. It's like preparing for battle, knowing the enemy's moves before they strike.

Troubleshooting Tip: If facing risks feels like stepping into a minefield, don't fret. We'll guide you through a risk assessment process.

Build a Cushion: The Power of Reserves

Step 2: Establish Financial Reserves
Think of financial reserves as your safety net—the cushion that softens the fall when unexpected expenses arise. Having reserves ensures that you're not caught off guard and can weather the storms that inevitably come with house flipping.

Troubleshooting Tip: If the idea of setting aside money for reserves seems challenging, we'll explore strategies to make it more manageable.

Diversify Your Investments

Step 3: Embrace Investment Diversification
Diversification is like having a well-balanced portfolio. Instead of putting all your eggs in one basket, spread your investments across different properties or projects. This strategy helps mitigate risks and ensures that the success of one flip can offset the challenges of another.

Troubleshooting Tip: If diversification feels like a financial puzzle, we'll break it down into simple pieces.

Key Takeaways

- Identify potential financial pitfalls through a thorough risk assessment.
- Establish financial reserves as a safety net for unexpected expenses.
- Embrace investment diversification to spread and manage risks.

Next Steps

1. Conduct a risk assessment. What potential pitfalls do you foresee?
2. Establish financial reserves. How much can you set aside for unforeseen expenses?
3. Explore investment diversification. How can you spread your investments across different properties or projects?

Congratulations! You're now equipped with strategies to manage financial risks in your house-flipping journey. The adventure continues in the next chapter, where we'll unravel the legal considerations and safeguards essential for a successful and compliant real estate venture!

Chapter 5

Navigating the Legal Landscape

Legal Considerations in House Flipping

Hello legal navigators! As we delve deeper into the world of house flipping, it's time to don our legal hats. This chapter is your guide through the legal intricacies and considerations that come with flipping properties. From permits to contracts, we'll ensure you sail through the legal seas unscathed.

The Permit Puzzle: Unraveling the Basics

Step 1: Understand the Importance of Permits
Permits are the foundation of a legally sound house flip. They ensure that your renovations comply with local regulations and safety standards. Understanding the permit process is like having a passport for your property improvements, it opens doors and keeps you on the right side of the law.

Troubleshooting Tip: If navigating the permit process feels like a maze, fret not. We'll provide a roadmap to guide you.

Contractual Confidence: The Power of Legal Agreements

Step 2: Master the Art of Contracts

Contracts are your legal shields. Whether dealing with contractors, real estate agents, or lenders, having solid legal agreements in place protects your interests. We'll explore the essential elements of contracts, ensuring you enter into agreements with confidence.

Troubleshooting Tip: If the thought of contracts makes your head spin, take a deep breath. We'll simplify the process.

Legal Safeguards: From Title Searches to Insurance

Step 3: Implement Comprehensive Legal Safeguards

Title searches, insurance, and inspections, these are your legal guardians. They shield you from potential headaches and financial disasters. We'll delve into the importance of each safeguard, ensuring your house-flipping venture is fortified against legal storms.

Troubleshooting Tip: If legal safeguards sound like a daunting fortress, fear not. We'll provide a blueprint for your legal defense.

Key Takeaways
- Permits are your passport to legally sound renovations.
- Contracts are your legal shields in various transactions.
- Legal safeguards, from title searches to insurance, provide comprehensive protection.

Next Steps
1. Understand the permit process in your local area.
2. Master the essentials of creating solid legal contracts.
3. Implement comprehensive legal safeguards for your house flips.

Congratulations! You're now armed with the legal knowledge needed to navigate the house-flipping landscape. The journey continues in the next chapter, where we'll explore the art of marketing and selling your renovated properties for maximum profit! Get ready to showcase your flipping masterpiece to the world!

Permits and Regulations

Greetings, legal navigators! In the realm of house flipping, understanding permits and regulations is like having a well-drawn treasure map, it leads you to the golden opportunities while avoiding potential pitfalls. This chapter is your guide to mastering the intricate dance of permits and regulations, ensuring your renovations comply with the law.

The Permit Primer: Why Permits Matter

Step 1: Grasp the Importance of Permits
Permits are the backstage pass to a successful and legal renovation. They ensure that your improvements meet safety standards and local regulations. Think of permits as your golden ticket, essential for a smooth journey through the renovation process.

Troubleshooting Tip: If the permit process feels like a bureaucratic puzzle, don't worry. We'll demystify it for you.

Navigating the Permit Maze: A Step-by-Step Guide

Step 2: Navigate the Permit Process
Now, let's break down the permit process into manageable steps. From initial research to submitting

applications, we'll guide you through the maze. Understanding each stage ensures that you obtain the necessary permits efficiently, keeping your project on track.

Troubleshooting Tip: If the permit process seems overwhelming, take a deep breath. We'll provide a roadmap for your journey.

Compliance Corner: Adhering to Local Regulations

Step 3: Adhere to Local Regulations

Every locality has its own set of regulations governing renovations. Understanding and adhering to these rules is crucial for a legally sound project. From zoning laws to building codes, we'll explore the regulatory landscape, helping you stay on the right side of the law.

Troubleshooting Tip: If deciphering local regulations feels like learning a new language, fear not. We'll provide a translation guide.

Key Takeaways
- Permits are your golden ticket to a legally sound renovation.
- Navigate the permit process step by step for efficiency.
- Adhere to local regulations to ensure compliance.

Next Steps

1. Grasp the importance of permits in your renovation projects.

2. Navigate the permit process step by step for efficiency.

3. Understand and adhere to local regulations governing your projects.

Congratulations! You're now equipped with the knowledge to navigate the permit and regulatory landscape of house flipping. The adventure continues in the next chapter, where we'll explore the art of marketing and selling your renovated properties for maximum profit! Get ready to showcase your flipping masterpiece to the world!

Contracts and Agreements

Hello legal maestros! As we continue our journey through the legal intricacies of house flipping, it's time to dive into the world of contracts and agreements. Think of these as the sturdy anchors that keep your ship steady in the sometimes turbulent waters of real estate transactions. This chapter is your guide to mastering the art of creating solid, legally binding contracts.

The Foundation: Understanding Contracts

Step 1: Grasp the Fundamentals of Contracts
Contracts are the building blocks of legal agreements. They outline the terms, responsibilities, and expectations of all parties involved in a transaction. Understanding the basics is like having a compass, it keeps everyone on the same path.

Troubleshooting Tip: If contracts seem like a legal labyrinth, don't fret. We'll break down the components into clear, actionable steps.

Crafting Your Shield: Elements of a Strong Contract

Step 2: Master the Essential Components
A strong contract is your legal shield. Whether dealing with contractors, real estate agents, or financial lenders,

your contract should leave no room for ambiguity. We'll explore the crucial elements that make a contract airtight and legally sound.

Troubleshooting Tip: If crafting contracts feels like walking on eggshells, worry not. We'll provide templates and guidance to ease the process.

The Power of Clarity: Avoiding Misunderstandings

Step 3: Embrace Clear and Concise Language
Ambiguity is the enemy of a good contract. Clear and concise language is your ally. We'll delve into the art of drafting language that leaves no room for misinterpretation, ensuring that all parties are on the same page.

Troubleshooting Tip: If the idea of legal language feels daunting, take a breath. We'll simplify the process

Key Takeaways
- Contracts are the foundation of legal agreements in house flipping.
- Master the essential components for crafting strong contracts.
- Embrace clear and concise language to avoid misunderstandings.

Next Steps

1. Grasp the fundamentals of contracts in real estate transactions.

2. Master the essential components for crafting strong and comprehensive contracts.

3. Embrace clear and concise language when drafting your agreements.

Congratulations! You're now well-versed in the art of creating solid contracts and agreements for your house-flipping ventures. The journey continues in the next chapter, where we'll explore the marketing and selling strategies to showcase your renovated properties for maximum profit! Get ready to unveil your flipping masterpieces to the world!

Think of these as the sturdy anchors that keep your ship steady in the sometimes turbulent waters of real estate transactions.

Chapter 6

Strategic Property Renovation

Creating a Renovation Plan

Greetings, renovation virtuosos! As we embark on the next leg of our house-flipping journey, it's time to roll up our sleeves and dive into the heart of the operation—the renovation plan. This chapter is your blueprint for crafting a strategic, efficient, and successful plan that transforms your property into a dazzling masterpiece.

The Foundation: Define Your Vision

Step 1: Clarify Your Renovation Vision
Before swinging hammers and picking paint colors, it's crucial to define your vision. What do you want the finished property to look like? Understanding your end goal is like having a North Star guiding every decision throughout the renovation process.

Troubleshooting Tip: If clarifying your vision feels like searching for a needle in a haystack, we'll help you pinpoint the key elements.

Budget Breakdown: Allocate Your Resources

Step 2: Establish a Comprehensive Budget
Budgeting is the backbone of any successful renovation plan. Break down your budget into categories such as materials, labor, and contingencies. This step ensures you allocate resources wisely, preventing financial surprises down the road.

Troubleshooting Tip: If the idea of budgeting makes you break into a cold sweat, fear not. We'll provide tools and strategies to make it more manageable.

Timeline Triumph: Set Realistic Deadlines

Step 3: Create a Realistic Timeline
Time is money in the world of house flipping. Set realistic deadlines for each phase of the renovation. This step not only keeps your project on track but also helps coordinate tasks efficiently, maximizing productivity.

Troubleshooting Tip: If creating a timeline feels like predicting the future, we'll guide you through the process.

Key Takeaways
- Clarify your renovation vision as the foundation of your plan.

- Establish a comprehensive budget to allocate resources effectively.
- Create a realistic timeline for efficient project coordination.

Next Steps

1. Clarify your vision for the renovated property. What do you want to achieve?
2. Establish a comprehensive budget, breaking down expenses into categories.
3. Create a realistic timeline for each phase of the renovation.

Congratulations! You're now armed with the essentials to create a strategic renovation plan for your house-flipping project. The adventure continues in the next chapter, where we'll explore the art of selecting materials and finishes to elevate your property's aesthetic appeal! Get ready to transform your vision into reality!

Budget-Friendly Upgrades

Hello budget-savvy renovators! In this chapter, we're diving into the art of creating stunning transformations without breaking the bank. Budget-friendly upgrades are the secret sauce to maximizing your property's appeal while keeping costs in check. Let's explore creative ways to elevate your flip without compromising on quality.

The Power of Paint: Transformative and Affordable

Step 1: Harness the Magic of Paint
Paint is your budget-friendly superhero. A fresh coat can breathe new life into any space, making it a go-to upgrade. From accent walls to kitchen cabinets, we'll explore how strategic paint choices can create a high-end look on a shoestring budget.

Troubleshooting Tip: If choosing the right paint feels like navigating a color maze, don't worry. We'll provide tips to simplify the process.

Revitalize with Refurbished Fixtures

Step 2: Embrace Refurbished Fixtures
Who says new is the only way to go? Refurbished fixtures, from lighting to hardware, can add character and style at a fraction of the cost. We'll guide you

through the world of second-hand treasures, helping you find the perfect pieces to enhance your space.

Troubleshooting Tip: If the idea of refurbishing feels overwhelming, relax. We'll share tips on spotting quality pieces and reviving them with ease.

Flooring Facelift: Affordable Elegance

Step 3: Explore Budget-Friendly Flooring Options
Flooring sets the foundation for a room's aesthetic, and budget-friendly options abound. From laminate to vinyl, we'll explore affordable flooring alternatives that mimic the look of high-end materials without the hefty price tag.

Troubleshooting Tip: If flooring choices seem like a maze, we'll simplify the decision-making process.

Key Takeaways
- Paint is a budget-friendly powerhouse for transformative upgrades.
- Refurbished fixtures add character and style at a fraction of the cost.
- Explore budget-friendly flooring options for an elegant finish.

Next Steps

1. Consider the transformative power of paint for your property.

2. Explore refurbished fixtures to add character and uniqueness.

3. Research budget-friendly flooring options to elevate your space.

Congratulations! You're now equipped with the knowledge to implement budget-friendly upgrades that enhance the appeal of your property without straining your finances. The journey continues in the next chapter, where we'll delve into the crucial aspect of marketing and selling your renovated property for maximum profit! Get ready to showcase your budget-friendly masterpiece to potential buyers!

Maximizing Curb Appeal

A visually captivating exterior not only draws potential buyers in but sets the tone for the entire renovation. Let's explore strategies to maximize curb appeal and make your property the star of the neighborhood.

Step 1: Harness the Power of Landscaping

Landscaping is the gateway to your property's personality. Well-maintained lawns, vibrant flowers, and strategic plantings create an inviting atmosphere. We'll delve into landscaping strategies that add charm without breaking the bank.

Troubleshooting Tip: If you have a brown thumb, fear not. We'll guide you through low-maintenance landscaping options.

Step 2: Elevate Your Front Door's Aesthetic

The front door is your property's handshake, it sets the tone for what's inside. Explore budget-friendly ways to upgrade your front door, from a fresh coat of paint to stylish hardware. We'll help you make a grand entrance without a grand budget.

Troubleshooting Tip: If choosing a front door style feels like a daunting decision, we'll provide inspiration and guidance.

Step 3: Illuminate Your Property Strategically

Outdoor lighting not only enhances safety but adds a touch of elegance. Explore budget-friendly lighting options to highlight architectural features and create a warm ambiance. We'll guide you through the process of illuminating your property like a nighttime masterpiece.

Troubleshooting Tip: If the world of outdoor lighting feels overwhelming, don't worry. We'll simplify the choices.

Key Takeaways

- Landscaping sets the stage for an inviting property.
- Upgrading the front door creates a memorable first impression.
- Strategic outdoor lighting adds elegance and enhances safety.

Next Steps

1. Evaluate your property's landscaping and consider improvements.
2. Explore budget-friendly upgrades for your front door.
3. Illuminate your exterior strategically with outdoor lighting.

Chapter 7

Project Management Essentials

Timeline and Milestone Planning

Greetings, project managers extraordinaire! As we delve into the heart of strategic property renovation, it's time to talk about the backbone of successful execution, timeline and milestone planning. This chapter is your guide to crafting a timeline that keeps your project on track and celebrates key milestones along the way.

Blueprint for Success: Crafting Your Timeline

Step 1: Develop a Comprehensive Project Timeline
Your project timeline is the roadmap that guides every nail hammered and paint stroke applied. Develop a comprehensive timeline that breaks down your renovation into phases, allocating realistic timeframes for each task. This step ensures efficient project coordination and a clear path to completion.

Troubleshooting Tip: If creating a timeline feels like predicting the weather, worry not. We'll provide templates and strategies to simplify the process.

Celebrate Progress: Identifying Key Milestones

Step 2: Identify and Celebrate Key Milestones
Milestones are the markers of progress, like signposts on your renovation journey. Identify key milestones, such as completing a room or reaching a specific phase, and celebrate these achievements. Acknowledging milestones not only boosts morale but also keeps the momentum going.

Troubleshooting Tip: If defining milestones feels like searching for hidden treasure, we'll help you pinpoint the significant moments in your project.

Flexibility in Action: Adapting to Changes

Step 3: Build Flexibility into Your Timeline
In the unpredictable world of renovations, flexibility is your secret weapon. Build buffer time into your timeline to accommodate unexpected delays or changes. This proactive approach ensures that you can navigate challenges without derailing your entire project.

Troubleshooting Tip: If the idea of flexibility makes you nervous, relax. We'll guide you on striking the right balance.

Key Takeaways

- Develop a comprehensive project timeline for efficient coordination.
- Identify and celebrate key milestones to boost morale.
- Build flexibility into your timeline to adapt to changes.

Next Steps

1. Develop a detailed timeline for your renovation project.
2. Identify key milestones to celebrate along the way.
3. Build flexibility into your timeline to accommodate unforeseen changes.

Congratulations! You're now equipped with the essentials of project management, ensuring your renovation progresses smoothly and reaches its triumphant conclusion. The adventure continues in the next chapter, where we'll explore effective marketing and selling strategies to showcase your renovated property to potential buyers! Get ready to unveil your project to the world!

Handling Unexpected Challenges

Hello, resilient project managers! In the unpredictable world of property renovation, challenges are inevitable. This chapter is your guide to navigating unexpected hurdles with grace and ensuring your project stays on course even when the renovation seas get a bit stormy.

Expecting the Unexpected: A Mindset Shift

Step 1: Adopt a Mindset of Resilience
The first line of defense against unexpected challenges is a resilient mindset. Embrace the reality that, in the world of renovations, surprises are par for the course. Shifting your perspective from "if" to "when" prepares you to face challenges head-on.

Troubleshooting Tip: If the idea of expecting the unexpected feels overwhelming, don't worry. We'll help you build mental resilience.

Crisis Mode: Swift and Calibrated Responses

Step 2: Develop a Crisis Response Plan
When challenges arise, having a crisis response plan in place is your superhero cape. Identify potential challenges that could derail your project and develop strategies to address them swiftly. This proactive

approach ensures you're ready to tackle issues head-on, minimizing their impact.

Troubleshooting Tip: If creating a crisis response plan feels like preparing for doomsday, fear not. We'll break it down into manageable steps.

Collaborative Problem-Solving: Engage Your Team

Step 3: Foster a Collaborative Problem-Solving Culture
In the face of challenges, a united front is your greatest asset. Foster a culture of collaborative problem-solving among your team members. Encourage open communication, creative thinking, and a shared commitment to finding solutions. A problem shared is a problem halved.

Troubleshooting Tip: If collaboration seems like a lofty ideal, we'll provide practical strategies to foster teamwork.

Key Takeaways
- Adopt a mindset of resilience to navigate unexpected challenges.
- Develop a crisis response plan for swift and calibrated reactions.
- Foster a collaborative problem-solving culture within your team.

Next Steps

1. Embrace a mindset of resilience in the face of unexpected challenges.

2. Develop a crisis response plan to address potential hurdles swiftly.

3. Foster a culture of collaborative problem-solving among your team members.

Congratulations! You're now armed with strategies to handle unexpected challenges like a seasoned project manager. The journey continues in the next chapter, where we'll explore effective marketing and selling strategies to showcase your renovated property to potential buyers! Get ready to turn challenges into triumphs!

Streamlining the Renovation Process

Hello efficiency aficionados! In this chapter, we'll embark on the journey of fine-tuning and optimizing your renovation process. Streamlining is the key to transforming your project into a well-choreographed symphony of productivity. Let's dive into the art of making every action count and every moment matter.

Strategic Choreography: Mapping Out Your Workflow

Step 1: Design a Strategic Workflow

Think of your renovation project as a carefully choreographed dance. Map out a strategic workflow, ensuring each task seamlessly transitions to the next. A well-designed workflow minimizes bottlenecks, enhances productivity, and keeps your project moving forward smoothly.

Troubleshooting Tip: If designing a workflow feels like untangling a knot, fret not. We'll provide a step-by-step guide to simplify the process.

Swift Decision-Making: Cutting Through the Noise

Step 2: Make Swift and Decisive Decisions

In the world of renovations, time is of the essence. Train yourself to make decisions swiftly and decisively.

Whether choosing materials, approving designs, or resolving issues, clear decision-making is the fuel that propels your project forward. We'll explore techniques to cut through the noise and make choices with confidence.

Troubleshooting Tip: If the idea of quick decision-making feels daunting, take a breath. We'll guide you through a decision-making framework.

Lean Principles: Trimming the Excess

Step 3: Embrace Lean Principles
In the spirit of efficiency, embrace lean principles to trim excess and eliminate waste. Identify areas where unnecessary steps or resources are slowing you down. Streamlining your process not only saves time but also ensures a more cost-effective and agile project.

Troubleshooting Tip: If the concept of lean principles seems unfamiliar, fear not. We'll break it down into actionable steps.

Key Takeaways
- Design a strategic workflow to optimize your renovation process.
- Make swift and decisive decisions to keep momentum.

- Embrace lean principles to trim excess and enhance efficiency.

Next Steps
1. Design a strategic workflow tailored to your renovation project.
2. Practice swift and decisive decision-making to maintain momentum.
3. Identify and eliminate excess steps using lean principles.

Congratulations! You're now equipped with the tools to streamline your renovation process and transform it into a well-orchestrated masterpiece. The adventure continues in the next chapter, where we'll explore effective marketing and selling strategies to showcase your optimized property to potential buyers! Get ready to unveil your streamlined creation to the world!

Streamlining is the key to transforming your project into a well-choreographed symphony of productivity.

Chapter 8

Effective Marketing Strategies

Developing a Compelling Listing

Hello marketing maestros! As we transition from the renovation phase to showcasing your masterpiece, it's time to delve into the art of effective marketing. This chapter will guide you through the process of creating a compelling listing that captivates potential buyers and sets the stage for a successful sale.

The Listing Blueprint: Crafting a Captivating Story

Step 1: Develop a Comprehensive Property Profile
Your listing is more than a collection of features, it's a story waiting to be told. Develop a comprehensive property profile that goes beyond the basics. Highlight the unique aspects of your renovated property, from its history to the thoughtful design choices you've made.

Troubleshooting Tip: If creating a property profile feels overwhelming, worry not. We'll break it down into manageable steps.

Visual Allure: High-Quality Photos and Virtual Tours

Step 2: Showcase Your Property with Stunning Visuals

A picture is worth a thousand words, especially in the world of real estate. Invest in high-quality photos and, if possible, virtual tours to showcase your property's aesthetic appeal. Potential buyers want to envision themselves in their future home, and compelling visuals make that imagination come to life.

Troubleshooting Tip: If navigating the world of photography feels like a challenge, we'll provide tips for stunning visuals.

Engaging Descriptions: Tell the Story

Step 3: Craft Engaging and Descriptive Listing Descriptions

Words matter. Craft engaging and descriptive listing descriptions that evoke emotion and paint a vivid picture. Use language that highlights the unique selling points of your property, creating an emotional connection with potential buyers.

Troubleshooting Tip: If writing descriptions feels like a daunting task, fear not. We'll provide templates and guidance to get you started.

Key Takeaways

- Develop a comprehensive property profile to tell a compelling story.
- Invest in high-quality photos and virtual tours for visual allure.
- Craft engaging and descriptive listing descriptions to create an emotional connection.

Next Steps

1. Develop a comprehensive property profile that goes beyond basic features.
2. Invest in high-quality photos and, if possible, virtual tours.
3. Craft engaging and descriptive listing descriptions to showcase your property's unique appeal.

Congratulations! You're now equipped with the essentials to create a compelling listing that captures the attention of potential buyers. The journey continues in the next chapter, where we'll explore effective selling strategies to close the deal and maximize your profits! Get ready to present your renovated property to the world!

Utilizing Social Media and Online Platforms

Hello digital trailblazers! In this chapter, we'll explore the dynamic world of social media and online platforms, an indispensable arena for marketing your renovated property. Let's dive into strategies to leverage the power of the internet to reach a broader audience and make your property stand out in the digital landscape.

Social Media Showtime: Choosing the Right Platforms

Step 1: Identify and Utilize Relevant Social Media Platforms

Not all social media platforms are created equal. Identify the ones most relevant to your target audience and the real estate market. Whether it's Instagram, Facebook, or Twitter, each platform has its strengths. Tailor your content to maximize engagement on each.

Troubleshooting Tip: If navigating social media platforms feels overwhelming, fear not. We'll provide insights into choosing the right ones for your property.

Visual Storytelling: Showcasing Your Property

Step 2: Harness the Power of Visual Content

Social media thrives on visuals. Showcase your property through visually appealing photos, virtual tours, and even videos. Visual storytelling not only captivates your audience but also allows them to experience the essence of your renovated property from the comfort of their screens.

Troubleshooting Tip: If creating visual content seems like a challenge, we'll provide tips and tools to make the process smoother.

Engaging with the Audience: Building Connections

Step 3: Foster Engagement and Interaction

Don't just broadcast, engage. Respond to comments, answer inquiries, and actively participate in online conversations. Building a community around your property creates a sense of connection and increases the likelihood of attracting potential buyers.

Troubleshooting Tip: If engaging with your audience feels daunting, we'll provide strategies to make it more manageable.

Key Takeaways

- Identify and utilize relevant social media platforms for your target audience.

- Harness the power of visual content to showcase your property online.
- Foster engagement and interaction to build a community around your listing.

Next Steps

1. Identify the social media platforms most relevant to your target audience.

2. Showcase your property through visually appealing content.

3. Foster engagement by actively participating in online conversations.

Congratulations! You're now equipped with the tools to navigate the digital landscape and utilize social media to market your renovated property effectively. The adventure continues in the next chapter, where we'll explore additional selling strategies to close the deal and turn your property into a buyer's dream! Get ready to shine in the online realm!

Attracting Potential Buyers

Greetings, property magnets! Now that your renovated masterpiece is ready for its grand debut, let's focus on attracting potential buyers. This chapter will guide you through strategies to make your property irresistible, ensuring it captivates the right audience and sparks the interest of eager buyers.

Step 1: Showcase Your Property's Allure

Curb appeal isn't just for physical properties, it matters online too. Ensure your online listings feature captivating visuals, showcasing the best angles of your property. Create a visual story that invites potential buyers to envision themselves living in the transformed space.

Troubleshooting Tip: If curating online appeal feels like a challenge, we'll guide to highlight your property's unique charm.

Step 2: Craft Compelling Listing Descriptions

Your listing description is more than a list of features; it's an invitation to a lifestyle. Use engaging language that not only highlights the property's attributes but also paints a vivid picture of the experience it offers. Sell not just the property but the dream of living in it.

Troubleshooting Tip: If crafting compelling descriptions seems daunting, fear not. We'll provide templates and tips to make it easier.

Step 3: Tailor Your Marketing to Your Ideal Buyer

Understanding your target audience is crucial. Tailor your marketing efforts to appeal directly to the desires and needs of your ideal buyer. Whether it's young professionals, families, or empty nesters, customize your approach to speak directly to the demographic that is most likely to be interested in your property.

Troubleshooting Tip: If defining your target audience feels like a puzzle, we'll guide you through the process.

Key Takeaways

- Showcase your property's allure through captivating online visuals.
- Craft compelling listing descriptions that sell the lifestyle.
- Tailor your marketing to appeal directly to your ideal buyer.

Next Steps

1. Enhance your online listings with captivating visuals.
2. Craft listing descriptions that sell the lifestyle, not just the features.
3. Tailor your marketing efforts to appeal directly to your target audience.

Chapter 9

Closing the Deal

Setting the Right Selling Price

Hello, deal closers! In this pivotal chapter, we'll tackle the art and science of setting the right selling price for your renovated property. Getting this crucial element right ensures that you attract potential buyers, maximize your profits, and smoothly navigate the negotiation phase.

Market Mastery: Understanding Comparable Sales

Step 1: Conduct a Thorough Market Analysis
Before determining your selling price, delve into the world of comparable sales. Analyze recent sales of similar properties in your area to understand the market trends. This step provides valuable insights into what buyers are willing to pay for homes with similar features and renovations.

Troubleshooting Tip: If navigating comparable sales feels like deciphering a secret code, don't worry. We'll guide you through the process.

Factoring in Renovations: Assessing Added Value

Step 2: Evaluate the Impact of Your Renovations
Your renovations are a key selling point, and they can add significant value to your property. Evaluate the impact of each renovation on the property's overall worth. Highlight the improvements that set your property apart and justify a higher selling price.

Troubleshooting Tip: If quantifying the value of renovations seems complex, we'll provide a straightforward approach.

Strategic Pricing: Attracting the Right Buyers

Step 3: Set a Competitive and Strategic Price
Balancing competitiveness and profitability is an art. Set a price that is competitive within the market while maximizing your potential profit. Strategic pricing attracts the right buyers and positions your property as a valuable investment.

Troubleshooting Tip: If deciding on the right price feels like a high-stakes gamble, we'll provide strategies to mitigate risks.

Key Takeaways

- Conduct a thorough market analysis to understand comparable sales.
- Evaluate the impact of your renovations on the property's value.
- Set a competitive and strategic selling price to attract the right buyers.

Next Steps

1. Dive into a market analysis to understand comparable sales in your area.
2. Assess the added value of your renovations to determine their impact on pricing.
3. Set a competitive and strategic selling price for your renovated property.

Congratulations! You're now armed with the knowledge to set the right selling price for your property, laying the foundation for a successful deal closing. The adventure continues in the next chapter, where we'll explore effective negotiation tactics to navigate the final steps of the selling process! Get ready to seal the deal with finesse!

Negotiating with Buyers

Greetings negotiation maestros! In this chapter, we're diving into the intricacies of negotiating with potential buyers, the final frontier before sealing the deal on your renovated property. Let's explore effective strategies to navigate this crucial phase with confidence and finesse.

Know Your Bottom Line: Setting Non-Negotiables

Step 1: Define Your Non-Negotiables
Before entering negotiations, establish your bottom line. Identify aspects of the deal that are non-negotiable, whether it's the selling price, specific terms, or timelines. Knowing your boundaries provides a solid foundation for a successful negotiation.

Troubleshooting Tip: If setting non-negotiables feels challenging, we'll guide you through the process.

Active Listening: Understanding Buyer Motivations

Step 2: Practice Active Listening
Understanding the buyer's motivations is a powerful negotiation tool. Actively listen to their concerns, preferences, and priorities. This insight allows you to tailor your responses and find mutually beneficial

solutions that address their needs while protecting your interests.

Troubleshooting Tip: If mastering active listening seems elusive, we'll provide practical techniques to enhance your skills.

Creative Problem-Solving: Finding Win-Win Solutions

Step 3: Foster a Collaborative Negotiation Atmosphere
Negotiation isn't a battle; it's a collaboration. Foster an atmosphere of collaboration by seeking win-win solutions. Creative problem-solving can lead to outcomes that satisfy both parties, creating a positive experience and increasing the likelihood of a successful deal.

Troubleshooting Tip: If navigating negotiations feels like walking on a tightrope, we'll provide strategies to keep your balance.

Key Takeaways
- Define your non-negotiables before entering negotiations.
- Practice active listening to understand the buyer's motivations.
- Foster a collaborative atmosphere for creative problem-solving.

Next Steps

1. Clearly define your non-negotiables for the negotiation process.

2. Practice active listening to understand the buyer's perspective.

3. Foster a collaborative atmosphere during negotiations to find win-win solutions.

Congratulations! You're now equipped with strategies to navigate negotiations with potential buyers effectively. The journey continues in the next chapter, where we'll explore the final steps of the closing process to officially hand over the keys and celebrate the successful sale of your renovated property! Get ready to finalize the deal with confidence!

Navigating the Closing Process

Hello, closing champions! In this chapter, we'll embark on the final steps of the journey, the closing process. Navigating this phase requires attention to detail, organization, and a touch of celebratory anticipation. Let's explore the key elements that ensure a smooth transition from negotiation to the official handover of your renovated property.

Dotting the I's and Crossing the T's: Due Diligence

Step 1: Complete Due Diligence Checklist

The closing process involves a meticulous checklist of tasks. From verifying title deeds to ensuring all necessary inspections are completed, due diligence is paramount. Ensure that all legal and administrative aspects are thoroughly addressed to avoid last-minute hiccups.

Troubleshooting Tip: If managing due diligence seems overwhelming, we'll guide you through a step-by-step checklist.

Finalizing the Paper Trail: Legal Documentation

Step 2: Review and Sign Legal Documents
As you approach the finish line, review and sign the legal documents required for the property transfer. This includes the sales contract, transfer deed, and any additional paperwork stipulated by local regulations. Ensuring accuracy in documentation is crucial for a seamless closing.

Troubleshooting Tip: If deciphering legal jargon feels like reading a foreign language, don't worry. We'll simplify the process.

Financial Formalities: Closing Costs and Payments

Step 3: Settle Closing Costs and Payments
The closing process involves settling financial matters, including closing costs, taxes, and any outstanding payments. Ensure that all financial transactions are executed smoothly to avoid delays in the final stages of the sale.

Troubleshooting Tip: If managing closing costs feels like navigating a maze, we'll provide a financial roadmap.

Key Takeaways

- Complete due diligence to address legal and administrative requirements.
- Review and sign the necessary legal documents for property transfer.
- Settle closing costs and financial transactions to finalize the sale.

Next Steps

1. Complete a thorough due diligence checklist for the closing process.
2. Review and sign all required legal documents for property transfer.
3. Settle closing costs and financial transactions to finalize the sale.

Congratulations! You're now prepared to navigate the closing process with confidence. The adventure concludes in the next chapter, where we'll celebrate the successful sale of your renovated property and explore ways to leverage this experience for future real estate endeavors. Get ready to raise a toast to your achievement!

Explore the key elements that ensure a smooth transition from negotiation to the official handover of your renovated property.

Chapter 10

Scaling Your House Flipping Business

Evaluating Your First Deal

Hello, budding real estate moguls! In this pivotal chapter, we'll shift gears from the specifics of a single deal to the broader strategy of scaling your house-flipping business. Let's dive into the critical process of evaluating your first deal, a foundational step in setting the stage for future success and growth.

Post-Project Reflection: Analyzing the Numbers

Step 1: Conduct a Comprehensive Financial Analysis
As you wrap up your first house flip, it's time to break out the calculator and analyze the numbers. Evaluate the financial performance of the project, including the total investment, renovation costs, and the final selling price. This analysis provides valuable insights into the profitability of your venture.

Troubleshooting Tip: If crunching numbers feel like a daunting task, don't worry. We'll guide you through the essential calculations.

Lessons Learned: Assessing Challenges and Successes

Step 2: Reflect on Challenges and Successes
Every project offers lessons. Take the time to reflect on the challenges you encountered and the successes you achieved. Were there unexpected hurdles? What strategies worked well? This reflection is a crucial step in refining your approach for future deals.

Troubleshooting Tip: If identifying lessons learned feels overwhelming, we'll provide prompts to guide your reflection.

Return on Investment: Calculating Your ROI

Step 3: Calculate Your Return on Investment (ROI)
The ROI is a key metric in determining the success of your house flip. Calculate the percentage return by comparing your profit to the total investment. Understanding your ROI not only gauges the success of the current project but also serves as a benchmark for future endeavors.

Troubleshooting Tip: If the concept of ROI seems elusive, fear not. We'll break it down into a straightforward formula.

Key Takeaways
- Conduct a comprehensive financial analysis to evaluate project profitability.
- Reflect on challenges and successes to extract valuable lessons.
- Calculate your Return on Investment (ROI) as a benchmark for future projects.

Next Steps
1. Conduct a detailed financial analysis of your first house flip.
2. Reflect on the challenges and successes encountered during the project.
3. Calculate your Return on Investment (ROI) to gauge overall project success.

Congratulations! You've successfully evaluated your first house flip, laying the groundwork for informed decisions as you scale your business. The journey continues in the next chapter, where we'll explore strategic approaches to scaling your house-flipping ventures. Get ready to elevate your real estate game!

Expanding Your Investment Portfolio

Hello ambitious investors! In this pivotal chapter, we're diving into the exhilarating world of expanding your investment portfolio. Whether you're a seasoned house flipper or just getting started, strategic expansion is the key to unlocking new opportunities and maximizing your success in the real estate market.

Visionary Goals: Setting the Stage for Expansion

Step 1: Define Clear Expansion Goals
Before charting the course for expansion, establish clear and visionary goals. What scale of growth are you aiming for? Are you looking to dominate a specific market, diversify your property types, or explore new geographic regions? Clearly defined goals provide the foundation for a successful expansion strategy.

Troubleshooting Tip: If setting goals feels daunting, we'll provide a structured approach to help you define your vision.

Market Mastery: Conducting Thorough Research

Step 2: Conduct Comprehensive Market Research
In the ever-evolving real estate landscape, knowledge is power. Conduct thorough market research to identify

lucrative opportunities. Analyze market trends, property values, and potential growth areas. This knowledge empowers you to make informed decisions and strategically expand your portfolio.

Troubleshooting Tip: If navigating market research seems complex, we'll simplify the process with practical guidance.

Diversification Magic: Spreading Your Wings

Step 3: Embrace Portfolio Diversification
Diversification is the secret sauce of a resilient investment portfolio. Explore opportunities to diversify your investments, whether it's by property type, location, or even exploring alternative real estate markets. Diversification helps mitigate risks and ensures your portfolio is well-positioned for sustained success.

Troubleshooting Tip: If diversification sounds like a puzzle, we'll provide a roadmap to help you achieve a well-balanced portfolio.

Key Takeaways
- Define clear and visionary goals for expanding your investment portfolio.
- Conduct comprehensive market research to identify lucrative opportunities.

- Embrace diversification to build a resilient and well-balanced portfolio.

Next Steps
1. Define specific and ambitious goals for expanding your investment portfolio.
2. Dive into comprehensive market research to gain insights into potential growth areas.
3. Explore opportunities for diversification to strengthen your investment portfolio.

Congratulations! You've now set the stage for strategic expansion, positioning yourself for greater success in the world of house flipping. The journey continues in the next chapter, where we'll explore effective management strategies to ensure the sustained growth and prosperity of your expanding real estate empire. Get ready to conquer new horizons!

Building Long-Term Success

Greetings, future real estate tycoons! In this concluding chapter, we'll explore the crucial aspect of building long-term success in your house-flipping venture. Beyond the immediate gains, the key to a flourishing real estate empire lies in strategic planning, continuous learning, and a commitment to sustained growth.

Legacy Building: Crafting Your Long-Term Vision

Step 1: Define Your Long-Term Vision
Building long-term success starts with envisioning your legacy. What do you want your real estate empire to look like in five, ten, or twenty years? Define your long-term vision, encompassing not just financial goals but also the impact you wish to make in the real estate industry.

Troubleshooting Tip: If visualizing your long-term vision feels challenging, we'll provide exercises to help you articulate your goals.

Continuous Learning: Staying Ahead of the Curve

Step 2: Commit to Continuous Education
The real estate landscape is dynamic, with trends and strategies evolving constantly. Commit to continuous learning to stay ahead of the curve. Whether it's staying updated on market trends, exploring innovative

renovation techniques, or understanding changing regulations, ongoing education is the foundation of long-term success.

Troubleshooting Tip: If finding time for continuous learning is a hurdle, we'll provide practical tips to integrate learning into your routine.

Strategic Adaptation: Flexibility in Action

Step 3: Embrace Strategic Adaptation
Long-term success requires the ability to adapt to changing circumstances. Stay flexible in your approach, be open to new opportunities, and adjust your strategies based on market dynamics. Strategic adaptation ensures that your business remains resilient and responsive to the evolving real estate landscape.

Troubleshooting Tip: If adapting to change feels challenging, we'll guide you through strategies to foster flexibility.

Key Takeaways
- Define a compelling long-term vision for your real estate empire.
- Commit to continuous education to stay informed and ahead of industry trends.

- Embrace strategic adaptation for resilience and sustained growth.

Next Steps
1. Clearly articulate your long-term vision for your house-flipping business.
2. Develop a plan for continuous learning to stay abreast of industry developments.
3. Foster a mindset of strategic adaptation to navigate the evolving real estate landscape.

Congratulations! You've now set the groundwork for building long-term success in your house-flipping journey. As you embark on this exciting path, remember that each project is not just a transaction but a building block in the creation of your real estate legacy. Best of luck on your journey to lasting prosperity!

Strategic adaptation ensures that your business remains resilient and responsive to the evolving real estate landscape.

Chapter 11

Common Pitfalls to Avoid

Learning from Mistakes

Greetings, seasoned and aspiring house flippers! In this enlightening chapter, we'll delve into common pitfalls to avoid in the intricate world of house flipping. Each misstep is an opportunity for growth, and by learning from these mistakes, you'll fortify your skills and increase your chances of long-term success in the real estate game.

Pitfall Awareness: Understanding Common Challenges

Step 1: Develop Awareness of Common Pitfalls
To navigate challenges effectively, you first need to identify them. From underestimating renovation costs to misjudging market trends, common pitfalls can significantly impact the success of your projects. Developing awareness is the first step towards proactive problem-solving.

Troubleshooting Tip: If recognizing pitfalls feels overwhelming, we'll provide real-world examples to illustrate common challenges.

Post-Project Reflection: The Power of Analysis

Step 2: Conduct Post-Project Reflection and Analysis

After each project, take a moment to reflect on the journey. What worked well? What challenges did you encounter? Analyzing your successes and mistakes provides valuable insights. It's not about blame but about learning and refining your approach for future projects.

Troubleshooting Tip: If reflecting on mistakes feels uncomfortable, we'll guide you through a constructive analysis process.

Risk Mitigation Strategies: Proactive Problem-Solving

Step 3: Develop Strategies for Risk Mitigation
Armed with the knowledge of common pitfalls, proactively develop strategies to mitigate risks. Whether it's building a buffer into your budget for unforeseen expenses or staying informed about market fluctuations, being prepared allows you to navigate challenges with resilience.

Troubleshooting Tip: If developing risk mitigation strategies feels complex, we'll provide a step-by-step guide to make it more manageable.

Key Takeaways

- Develop awareness of common pitfalls in the house-flipping process.
- Conduct post-project reflection and analysis to learn from mistakes.
- Proactively develop strategies for risk mitigation to enhance project success.

Next Steps

1. Develop a keen awareness of common pitfalls in house flipping.
2. Conduct thorough post-project reflection and analysis.
3. Proactively develop strategies for risk mitigation to enhance project success.

Congratulations! By embracing the lessons embedded in mistakes, you're not just avoiding pitfalls; you're transforming challenges into stepping stones toward a more refined and successful house-flipping journey. The adventure continues in the next chapter, where we'll explore effective ways to market your properties for maximum impact and profitability. Get ready to shine in the real estate spotlight!

Overcoming Challenges

Hello, resilient real estate enthusiasts! In this chapter, we'll embark on a journey to tackle challenges head-on and emerge victorious in the ever-dynamic world of house flipping. By adopting a proactive mindset and implementing strategic solutions, you'll not only overcome adversities but also fortify your foundation for enduring success.

Proactive Mindset: Embracing Challenges as Opportunities

Step 1: Adopt a Proactive Mindset
Challenges are not roadblocks but growth opportunities. Embrace a proactive mindset that sees each obstacle as a chance to learn, innovate, and strengthen your house-flipping skills. By reframing challenges as stepping stones, you'll navigate the real estate landscape with resilience.

Troubleshooting Tip: If adopting a proactive mindset seems daunting, we'll provide practical exercises to shift your perspective.

Strategic Problem-Solving: Analyzing and Addressing Issues

Step 2: Implement Strategic Problem-Solving Techniques

When challenges arise, strategic problem-solving is your ally. Analyze the root causes of issues, break them down into manageable components, and develop targeted solutions. This methodical approach allows you to address challenges with precision and efficiency.

Troubleshooting Tip: If strategic problem-solving feels overwhelming, we'll guide you through a step-by-step process.

Building a Support Network: Collaboration and Advice

Step 3: Cultivate a Robust Support Network

You don't have to face challenges alone. Cultivate a support network that includes experienced mentors, industry professionals, and fellow house flippers. Drawing on collective wisdom and seeking advice from those who've faced similar challenges can provide invaluable insights and solutions.

Troubleshooting Tip: If building a support network feels challenging, we'll provide strategies to connect with like-minded individuals in the industry.

Key Takeaways

- Adopt a proactive mindset, viewing challenges as opportunities for growth.
- Implement strategic problem-solving techniques to address issues effectively.
- Cultivate a robust support network for guidance and collaboration.

Next Steps

1. Embrace a proactive mindset in the face of challenges.
2. Implement strategic problem-solving techniques to address specific issues.
3. Cultivate a robust support network for guidance and collaboration.

Congratulations! By embracing challenges as stepping stones and cultivating a proactive approach, you're not just overcoming adversities; you're thriving in the dynamic world of house flipping. The journey continues in the next chapter, where we'll explore effective marketing strategies to elevate the visibility and desirability of your properties. Get ready to showcase your real estate prowess!

Staying Informed on Market Trends

Greetings, savvy real estate navigators! In this chapter, we'll delve into the importance of staying informed on market trends, a vital aspect of thriving in the dynamic world of house flipping. By keeping a finger on the pulse of market shifts, you'll make informed decisions, seize opportunities, and ensure your house-flipping endeavors remain on the cutting edge.

Trend Spotting: The Power of Market Awareness

Step 1: Cultivate a Keen Sense of Market Awareness
To navigate the ever-evolving real estate landscape, cultivate a keen sense of market awareness. Stay attuned to emerging trends, shifts in buyer preferences, and changes in local market dynamics. Being proactive in trend-spotting positions you as a forward-thinking house flipper.

Troubleshooting Tip: If developing market awareness feels challenging, we'll provide strategies to streamline the process.

Industry Insights: Utilizing Resources for Information

Step 2: Leverage Industry Resources for Insights

Tap into industry resources, including real estate publications, online forums, and market reports. These sources provide valuable insights into current trends, regional market conditions, and projections for future developments. By leveraging these resources, you'll make well-informed decisions that align with market realities.

Troubleshooting Tip: If navigating industry resources seems overwhelming, we'll guide you through the most valuable channels.

Networking Power: Collaborating with Industry Professionals

Step 3: Engage in Networking to Stay Informed

Networking isn't just about building connections; it's a powerful tool for staying informed. Attend industry events, join real estate associations, and connect with professionals in your field. Engaging in conversations with fellow house flippers, real estate agents, and industry experts provides on-the-ground insights that go beyond data.

Troubleshooting Tip: If networking feels challenging, we'll provide tips to make it more approachable.

Key Takeaways

- Cultivate a keen sense of market awareness for trend-spotting.
- Leverage industry resources for insights into current market dynamics.
- Engage in networking to stay informed through real-world experiences.

Next Steps

1. Develop a habit of observing and analyzing market trends.
2. Utilize industry resources to gather insights into current market conditions.
3. Expand your network by engaging with professionals in the real estate industry.

Congratulations! By staying informed on market trends, you're not just a participant in the real estate market; you're a trendsetter. The journey continues in the next chapter, where we'll explore strategic financial planning to ensure the profitability and sustainability of your house-flipping ventures. Get ready to navigate the financial landscape with confidence!

Conclusion

Congratulations, House Flipping Maestro! You've embarked on a transformative journey, navigating the twists and turns of the dynamic real estate realm. As you reach the final pages of "How to Flip Houses for Massive Profits," reflect on the wealth of knowledge, strategies, and insights gained along the way.

In these chapters, you've not only learned the art of securing lucrative deals, transforming properties, and negotiating with finesse, but you've also mastered the crucial skill of learning from challenges. Every stumble has become a stepping stone, and every setback a setup for a grand comeback.

Your house-flipping venture is not just a business; it's a canvas for your creativity, a stage for your resilience, and a pathway to financial success. By defining your investment goals, assembling a stellar team, and embracing the ebb and flow of market trends, you've become a true architect of your real estate destiny.

As you close this chapter, remember that the journey doesn't end here; it evolves. The keys to long-term success lie in continuous learning, strategic adaptation, and staying ahead of market trends. Whether you're a seasoned flipper expanding your empire or a novice stepping into the thrilling world of house flipping, your potential is limitless.

Seal the deal with confidence, embrace challenges as opportunities, and let your passion for real estate fuel your success. Your story as a house flipper is just beginning, and the next chapter is waiting to be written.

Thank you for joining us on this exhilarating house-flipping odyssey. May your projects be profitable, your renovations be flawless, and your real estate empire be boundless. Here's to your success, your growth, and the exciting ventures that lie ahead.

Happy flipping, and may every flip be your best one yet!